Birds
of the countryside

Illustrated by A. Oxenham

based on the Thames Television Series

LUTTERWORTH PRESS LONDON

Introduction

In a book about birds we should first be clear what we mean by "a bird". In what way is a bird different from all other living creatures? You might immediately think it is because it can fly – but many insects fly and a few birds (such as the emu) cannot. You might think it is because it lays eggs – but so do many reptiles; or because it makes a nest – but so do many mammals. No, it is because it has feathers; all birds have feathers but no other creatures do.

This book is about "wild birds" – in other words, those which live their lives in a natural state; it does not include cage birds, though of course all cage birds descended from wild birds originally. In Britain there are something like 100 million wild birds – about two to every human being. Altogether, 455 species (kinds) of birds have been recorded in Britain; some of these, like the robin, are with us all the time, some, like the house martin, come just for the summer or for the winter, while others are "vagrants" which have strayed from other countries.

British birds vary greatly in size – from the goldcrest, only 3½ inches long and 1/6th of an ounce in weight, to the mute swan, 5 feet long and 30 lb. in weight; incidentally, the mute swan is the world's largest flying bird. Shapes vary, too – from the stubby little wren, poking around dead leaves, to the graceful avocet, probing for food in the mud of an estuary; there are long bills, short bills, slender feet, webbed feet, narrow wings, squarish wings – many shapes and sizes. And, of course, there is a great variety of colour. This book shows you some of the shapes, sizes and colours which make birds so distinctive and so fascinating to watch. But it is not only these features which make bird-watching an excellent hobby. A great thing about birds is that you can watch them anywhere – in town or country, on a mountain-top or at sea. Also, there is always the exciting possibility of a rare bird suddenly appearing – even in your own garden.

You can do much to attract birds to your garden – putting out the right food, supplying a bird bath, making nest boxes, etc. Then, you will want to go further afield. You will probably find many good places not far from your home – reservoirs, parks, woods; holidays to the sea or mountains provide great possibilities. Bird-watching is an adventure – anywhere.

Robin

House Martin

four of Britain's
biggest birds
Capercaillie
Golden Eagle
Canada Goose
Mute Swan

four of Britain's smallest birds
Goldcrest
Wren
Coal Tit
Chiffchaff

Archaeopteryx

evolution

There have been birds in the world for about 150 million years – a long time compared with man's half million years. Like all other animals, birds did not suddenly appear, but are the result of the slowly changing process of evolution. From the evidence of fossils, it appears that birds evolved from reptiles.

The first known bird was *Archaeopteryx*. Its most important feature was that it had feathers, which developed from reptile scales. As its wing muscles were weak, it could not have been able to fly much; in fact, it was probably only capable of simple, gliding flight. Its tail was long and flat, and its legs strong. It had the wish-bone which modern birds have, but it also had teeth. *Archaeopteryx* was probably descended from tree-climbing lizard-like animals with long tails, which they used for balancing; the gradual change from scales to feathers on the front legs (later to become "wings") would enable them to leap more easily from branch to branch.

Feathers and wings provided birds with the great advantage of flight. As birds evolved, their wings became more efficient; different species gradually developed with very different wings – some for rapid, dashing flight, some for long distances and some for soaring.

Also other parts – bills, feet and tails – developed in a variety of shapes and sizes, all suited to their particular needs. For instance, the bullfinch's short, stubby bill is ideal for eating seeds and buds, whereas the curlew's long curved one enables it to probe deeply in the mud. Most birds have three toes in front and one behind, but woodpeckers have two in front and two behind, enabling them to climb trees; many swimming birds, such as the mallard, have webbed feet.

All these 'adaptations' offer advantages to the birds concerned.

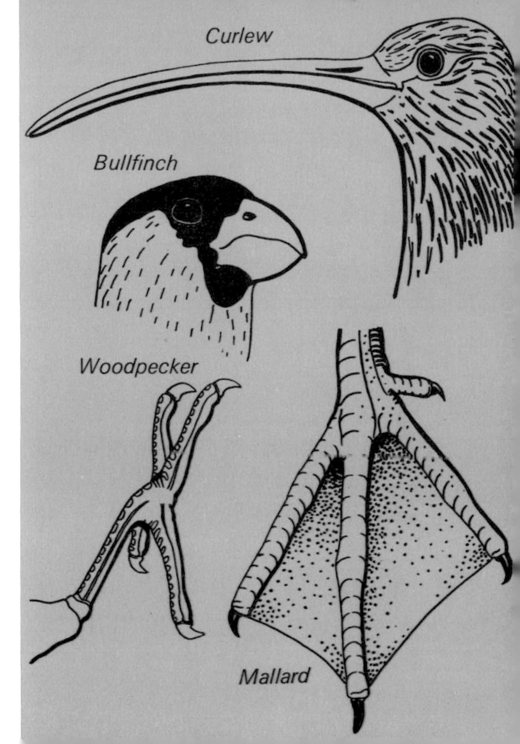

garden birds

Great Tit
Song Thrush
Blue Tit
Mistle Thrush
Chaffinch

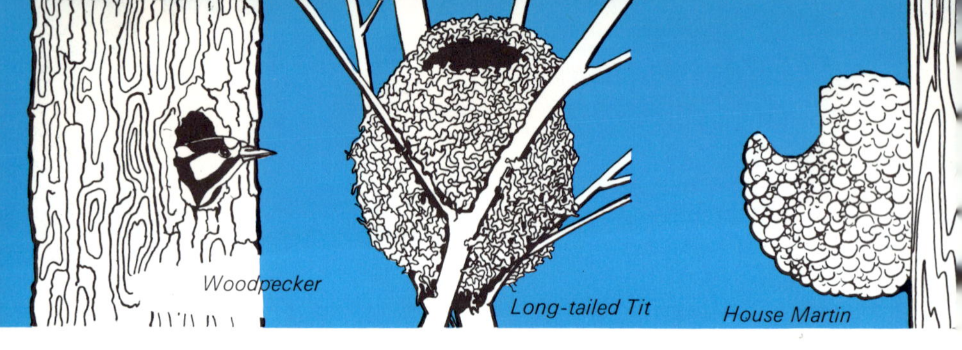

nests

Birds' nests serve mainly as places for laying and incubating eggs and, often, also as a home for the young until they can fly. In the same way as there is such variety in the shapes and sizes of birds, so is there also in their nests.

Probably the best-known type is cup-shaped, such as a blackbird builds in a hedge or bush, using mainly grass and moss, solidified with mud. Also cup-shaped, but made almost entirely of mud, with a lining of straw and feathers, is that of a swallow; it is usually on a beam or ledge in a barn or out-building. A house martin builds a rather similar nest but up against the eaves of a house, with just a small opening at the top.

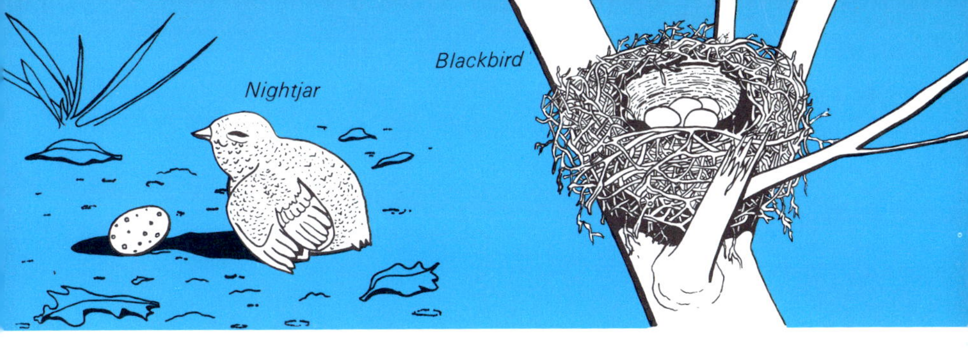

A long-tailed tit builds a complicated domed nest, made of finely woven moss, cobwebs and hair. Woodpeckers bore holes in trees and use only a few chips of wood as nest material. Many other hole-nesting birds, on the other hand, use existing holes – like a blue tit, which builds a nest of grass and moss lined with hair or feathers, or a nuthatch which plasters the entrance hole with mud to reduce its size; both these birds will use nestboxes. Some birds do not build at all. For instance, a nightjar just lays its eggs in a scrape in the ground, and a guillemot on bare rock.

It is against the law to take or damage birds' nests while they are being used. However, it is permissible, and very interesting, to collect them and examine them in the autumn.

woodland birds

Jay

Tawny Owl

Great Spotted Woodpecker

Green Woodpeck

Lesser Spott
Woodpecker

Blackcap
Redstart
Nightingale
Nuthatch

Breaking out of the shell

Day-old blackbird

from egg to bird

All birds lay eggs but the number varies enormously – from the single egg of a guillemot to the 20 or more of a pheasant or partridge; typical of garden birds are the blackbird's 3 to 5 and the blue tit's 7 to 14. The size varies from the mute swan's egg of $4\frac{1}{2}$ inches long to that of the goldcrest of only about $\frac{1}{2}$ inch long. And, of course, the colours vary greatly, too; the eggs of birds with very exposed nests, such as a ringed plover, often appear to be camouflaged to blend in with the surroundings, while some hole-nesting birds, such as tawny owls, lay white eggs.

Birds' eggs are indeed very beautiful things and are tempting to collect. However, egg-collecting is now against the law and this includes taking even just one egg from common birds such as blackbirds, robins, song thrushes and blue tits. And, when you think of it, it would be stupid for anyone who is genuinely interested in birds and their protection to take away their eggs!

As you know, a newly-laid egg consists mainly of the yolk and the "white" or albumen. On the yolk is a small germ cell which eventually develops into the chick, and the yolk supplies nutriment for this; the albumen serves as a sort of cushion and also supplies some nutriment. For the fertilized eggs to develop into chicks, they must be kept at a certain temperature, and warmth is provided by the parents sitting on them; this "incubation" period varies with different species, but for most song birds it is about 2 weeks.

On hatching, most birds are quite helpless and naked, but they rapidly increase in size and grow feathers. Young blackbirds leave the nest after 2 weeks, young blue tits after nearly 3 weeks. For some time after this, they are fed by their parents. Some birds, on the other hand, are already covered with down when hatched and can run out of their nest almost immediately. These are mainly ground-nesting birds – ducks, geese and waders.

Observing the parents feeding young birds – in or out of the nest – is a rewarding pastime.

Day-old mallard

Feeding fledged blackbirds

farmland
birds
Wood pigeon
Skylark
Lapwing
Linnet

Magpie
Yellowhammer
Rook
Partridge

feeding

No two species of birds have exactly the same diet and feeding habits. This reduces competition between species, particularly when food is scarce, and is a means to survival.

These differences are achieved in several ways. First of all, birds have different "habitats" (types of country or surroundings) which they prefer. For instance, kingfishers live near water and woodpeckers live near trees. Secondly, some birds feed mainly on the ground (blackbirds and dunnocks), some mainly on trees and bushes (blue tits and nuthatches), some in water (herons and mallard) and some in the air (swallows and house martins). Thirdly, within these four – ground, trees, water and air – there are further variations. Different ground-feeders prefer different sorts of ground (open field, undergrowth, etc). Similar species feeding on trees may choose different levels; Mallard feed in shallow water, while tufted ducks feed in deeper water. In the air, spotted flycatchers dart for insects from low branches, while swifts often give chase high above the roof-tops.

Beak shapes vary greatly according to the bird's diet. For example, most insect eaters have thin, pointed beaks (flycatchers), whereas seed eaters have short, stubby cone-shaped ones (greenfinch). Birds which probe in the ground have long bills (woodcock). A heron has a dagger-like bill for spearing fish. A green woodpecker has a strong, sharp bill, for boring into wood and also an extremely long tongue for extracting insects from holes.

Fish eater – Heron

Boring for insects – Golden Woodpecker

freshwater birds

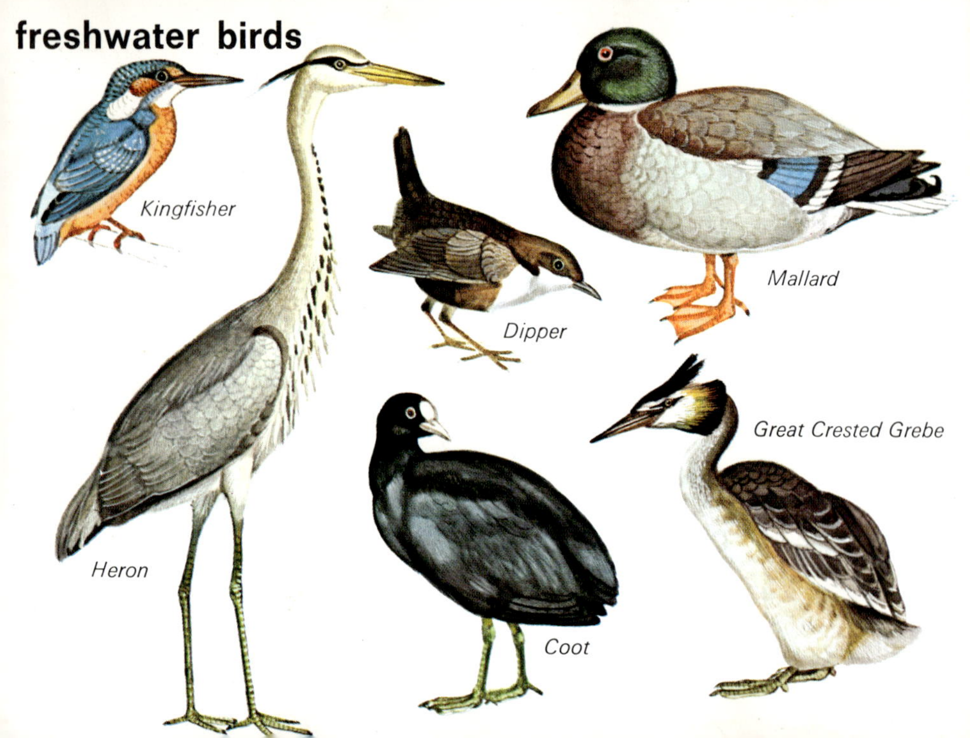

sea birds
Eider
Gannet
Puffin
Cormorant
Great Black-backed Gull
Fulmar

migration

Although many birds, such as robins and blackbirds, are with us all the year round, others come to Britain only for the summer or for the winter. Summer visitors include the swallow, house martin, cuckoo, spotted flycatcher and turtle dove; while in Britain they breed, and then afterwards they and their young move to warmer climates further south. There are also winter visitors, which include redwing, waxwing, and several species of ducks, geese and swans; these are birds which breed in colder climates (Greenland, Iceland, Scandinavia) and, just like our summer visitors, move to a warmer climate for the winter. In addition to these summer and winter visitors, there are "passage migrants" which breed further north and winter further south, just passing through Britain on the way. Also, some members of our resident species, including robins and starlings, move in and out of Britain during winter and summer.

The basic reason for migration is that it enables the birds to keep in the climate which is suitable for the food supply that they require. For instance, when autumn comes, there are not sufficient flying insects in Britain to keep swallows alive, so the swallows must go elsewhere. They go to South Africa, and so each year they have two summers.

The distances travelled on migration are often very great. Swallows, going to South Africa and back, do a round trip of about 10,000 miles. The greatest traveller, however, is the arctic tern, which breeds in the arctic and goes to

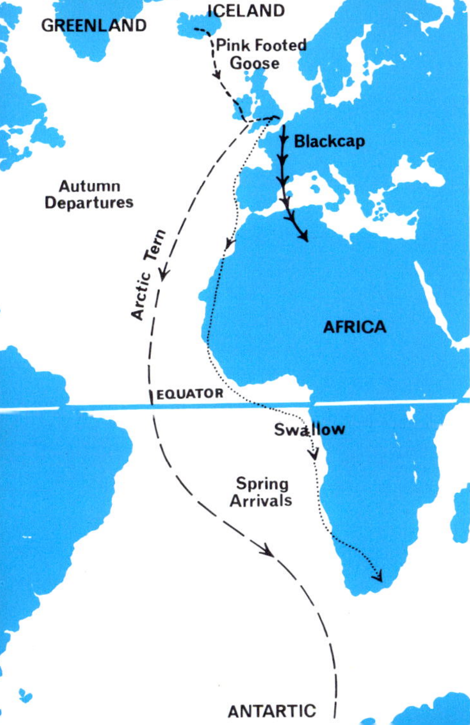

the antarctic during our winter – a round trip of up to 22,000 miles a year. Our information about routes and distances is obtained from "ringing" birds with numbered rings. Before embarking on these long migration journeys, the birds eat a great deal and increase the amount of fat on their bodies, so giving themselves a store of energy. Some species, such as the sedge warbler, actually double their body-weight before departure.

How birds can find their way over such long distances has always been a mystery, and it is by no means completely solved. It is thought that they navigate by the sun and stars, using a sort of built-in clock. This must be done by instinct because young cuckoos, for instance, leave Britain after the adults have gone. Migration is indeed a marvel of nature.

summer visitors
Turtle Dove
Cuckoo
Swallow
Spotted
Flycatcher
Arctic Tern

winter visitors

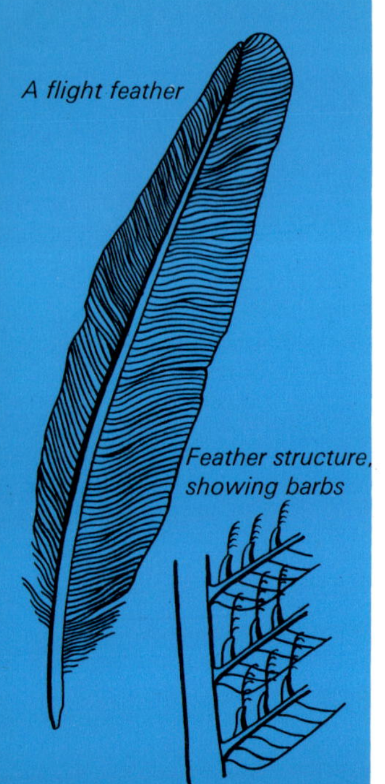

feathers and flight

As already mentioned, it is having feathers that makes birds different from all other living creatures. Feathers enable them to fly, keep their bodies warm, and are used for camouflage and display.

Birds have two main types of feathers: long, strong ones on their wings, tails and the outside of their bodies; inner small, downy ones which provide extra insulation. As birds have higher body temperatures than humans (106° F. instead of 98° F.), insulation is extremely important; in cold weather they often "fluff themselves out" to trap more warm air inside. The number of feathers increases with the size of the bird – from about 2,000 on a small song bird to about 25,000 on a swan. A flight or outer body feather has a central shaft and a vein consisting of hundreds of parallel spikes ("barbs"). Each barb, like a miniature feather, has smaller barbs with hooks, and the whole structure locks together. The care of feathers is obviously very important, and birds spend much time bathing and preening.

A bird is an extremely efficient flying machine – far better than any aeroplane. Apart from normal flapping flight, there is the gliding flight of a gull, the soaring of a buzzard, the diving of a peregrine or a gannet, the hovering of a kestrel and, above all, numerous aerobatics which can only be caught with a high-speed camera.

Birds have a variety of wing shapes to suit their special needs. A buzzard's squarish wings are suited for soaring, a gull's long, narrow ones for gliding, whereas a swift's swept-back wings are designed for speed and manoeuvrability.

As regards speed, most small birds probably usually fly at 20–30 m.p.h., larger ones up to 60 m.p.h. A speed of 100 m.p.h. has been claimed for swifts, but accurate timing is difficult.

birds of prey

The birds of prey cover two groups of birds: firstly, eagles, hawks, falcons and buzzards, which feed by day; secondly, owls, most of which feed by night. All these birds have two things in common: strong talons for carrying and holding the food, and hooked beaks for tearing it into pieces small enough to swallow. Their food varies but includes mammals (mice, rats, rabbits, etc.), birds, fish and insects. They actually benefit these species by killing the sick or weak.

Methods of hunting vary greatly. Peregrines dive("stoop")at great speeds on to flying birds; sparrowhawks flit between trees; kestrels hover; harriers and owls fly slowly while quartering the ground. This explains why birds of prey have such varied wing shapes.

Barn Owl

Little Owl

Short-eared O

Merlin
Sparrowhawk
Peregrine
Kestrel
Buzzard

bird song

Bird song has attracted man for a very long time, and much poetry – and music – has been written about it. Yet, it is something which in this busy world we tend to take for granted. Have you really listened to the birds? A good time to start is the dawn chorus. One spring morning, get up well before dawn, and wait, quietly, until you hear the first bird sing; then, as the sky gradually lightens, listen as more and more start to sing, swelling into a magnificent chorus. It is an experience you will never forget.

The songs and calls of birds are excellent aids to recognition; indeed, a good bird-watcher walking through a wood will probably identify far more birds by sound than by sight. The best way to learn bird sounds is to go out with an expert; but gramophone records are also a great help, and there are now some excellent bird song records on the market.

The main purposes of bird song seem to be to claim a territory and to attract a mate; this explains why

Mistle Thrush

bird song is greatest in spring. The song must of course be heard, so it is repeated over and over again, often from high branches or television aerials. Birds have a vocabulary of calls, which are used as signals for danger, food supply, etc.

Some young birds (e.g. nightingales) learn their songs from others of their species, but other birds (e.g. swallows) inherit their songs and would instinctively know their own songs even if isolated from all other swallows. Some birds also mimic the songs and calls of others; the starling is the best-known and has been heard to mimic even farmyard chickens and telephone bells!

The great variety of bird song is truly wonderful, and it has been suggested recently that it was from the birds that man learnt to sing and make music. Certainly, when man first entered the world, birds had been here, and undoubtedly singing, for many millions of years.

Today many people make a hobby of recording bird song, an activity which can be both entertaining and instructive.

Owl

rare birds

By a rare bird we usually do not mean a species of which there are only a few hundred birds left in the world. What we really mean are birds which only occur in Britain in small numbers, though they may be quite common elsewhere; in the same way, some common British birds would be considered "rare" in America. There are many birds which do not breed in Britain but which have been observed only occasionally, possibly when blown off course by storms. But the rare birds which are pictured here all breed in Britain. The osprey, snowy owl, avocet and black-tailed godwit had all ceased to breed in Britain, but have all started to do so again in small numbers, helped by the Royal Society for the Protection of Birds.

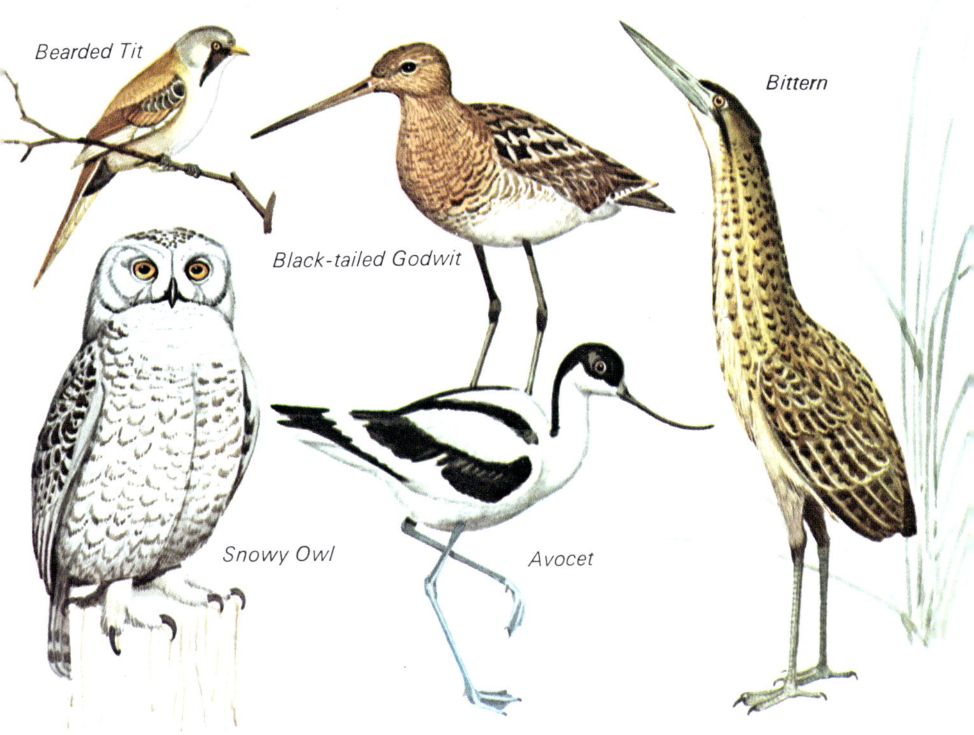
Bearded Tit
Black-tailed Godwit
Bittern
Snowy Owl
Avocet

conservation

By "conservation" we mean "the wise use of our natural resources" which include soil, rocks, minerals and water as well as the countryside and all the animals and plants it contains. It is "nature conservation" – the countryside and its wildlife – that we, as bird-watchers, are concerned with.

The countryside is decreasing all the time – towns expand, new factories go up, and more motorways and airports are built. In the country, farming is becoming more intensive – grassland is ploughed up, hedges cut down and poisonous chemicals are used on a wide scale. Also, people these days have more leisure (as the five-day week becomes more general) and more people have cars, so an increasing number go to the country each weekend – picnicing, camping, sailing and fishing. And of course there are more people – our population is increasing. All these things mean that there are fewer undisturbed places for birds and other animals to live in. That is why, nature conservation is so important.

There are several large organisations dealing with nature conservation. Firstly, there is the Nature Conservancy, the Government body which has reserves and does research. Then there are Naturalists' Trusts in every county in England and Wales, and in Scotland there is the Scottish Wildlife Trust. Specially concerned with birds is The Royal Society for the Protection of Birds. The R.S.P.B. has forty birds reserves, and has a special organisation for boys

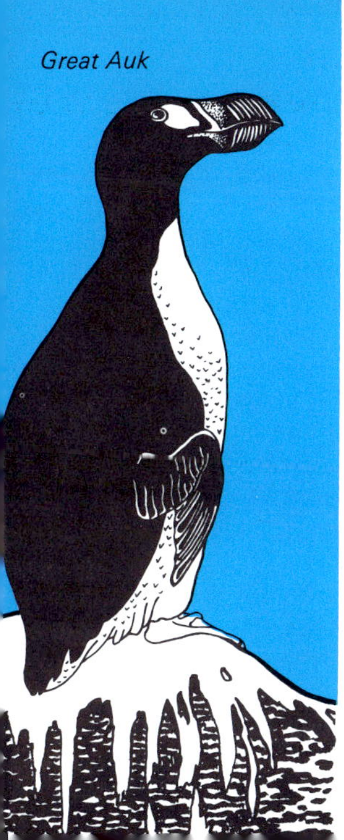
Great Auk

and girls – The Young Ornithologists' Club (The Lodge, Sandy, Bedfordshire) which runs courses and outings, organises projects and surveys, and publishes its own magazine *Bird Life*.

There are several different sorts of work carried out on bird reserves. On some, rare species are protected – such as ospreys at Loch Garten, and avocets on Havergate Island, Suffolk. In many it is the protection of a habitat which is important – particularly reed-beds and marshes. Also, reserves have to be "managed" – they are not just fenced in and left; scrub has to be cut, reeds cut back so as to leave clear water, and in some cases artificial lakes are constructed with islands for avocets and terns.

What can *you* do to help nature conservation? You can visit reserves, you can improve your garden for birds (as described in the next few pages), and you can join the Young Ornithologists' Club and so learn more about birds and the dangers threatening them.

The great auk became extinct in 1844 because of man's thoughtlessness; if we are not careful, many other species will follow it.

bird tables

Here is a bird table which you can easily make yourself for only a few shillings. The materials you need are: a 12″ × 18″ piece of exterior (or marine) plywood, $\frac{1}{2}$″ thick; a 4′ 4″ length of 1″ × 1″ wood; a dozen 1$\frac{1}{4}$″ brass screws or galvanized nails; also a means of supporting or hanging the bird table. To make the wood last longer, treat it with preservative.

In order to prevent food from being blown off the table and yet to allow water to drain off, cut the 1″ × 1″ wood into two 12″ lengths and two 14″ lengths, and fix these along the top edges of the plywood, leaving a gap of about 1″ at each corner. Screw right through the plywood from below. If you use nails, beware of splitting the wood.

Your bird table can either be supported on a post or hung from a branch. To hang it, screw small brass or galvanized screw-eyes into the wooden strips at each corner of the bird table. To each of these attach equal lengths (about 2 feet) of terylene or nylon cord, and tie the cords to a bough.

For a wooden post, 2″ × 2″ is ideal – 5 feet high with an extra foot or so to drive into the ground. Having driven in the post, the difficult part is attaching the table to it. You can either screw four metal angle brackets to the table and post; or, better still, you can form a square recess under the table to take the post, using short lengths of 2″ × 1″ wood screwed through the table from the top and screwed to each other, fixing these to the post with a screw at each side.

providing food and water

If you put out food for the birds in your garden, you will attract more of them and may help them in hard weather when their natural foods are scarce. Whether you have a bird table or not, you can feed the birds and, in fact, even if you do have one, you should still put some food on the ground for birds such as dunnocks and blackbirds which prefer to feed there.

Many kitchen scraps are suitable: cake crumbs, bread crusts, meat bones, ham skin, chopped bacon rind, cooked potato, raw pastry, cheese rind, apple cores. For seed-eaters, you can buy wild bird mixtures such as "Swoop". Peanuts are a great favourite with tits and greenfinches, and you can either buy these shelled and put them into a nut basket or plastic "stocking" (of the sort in which fruit is often sold in supermarkets) or buy them unshelled for threading on to fine string. Coconut is also much liked in cold weather; buy a whole coconut, split into two halves and hang "meat" downwards. Never give desiccated coconut as this may swell up inside the bird's stomach.

It is unnecessary to put out food in spring and summer; in fact, it could be a bad thing to do so as birds might not give their young the right diet. Winter is the right time, but do not feed, then suddenly stop in a cold spell, because the birds may have become dependent on your supply.

Birds also need water. The ideal is a pond, and you can easily make one with polythene sheeting, preferably the thick, black type. Just dig a hole, sprinkle in some sand or fine soil, line with polythene, anchor its edges with stones or turf, and fill with water. If you do not have room for a pond, an upturned dustbin lid, preferably of the rubber or plastic type, makes a good substitute; put some stones in the middle.

By providing food and water, you will attract more birds to your garden, and you will do something towards conservation. It is an excellent idea to keep a daily record of the different kinds of birds that you attract in this way. The variety you see may come as a surprise.

how to make a nestbox

This nestbox is specially designed for those with no carpentry skill and few tools. It will attract hole-nesting birds such as blue tits and nuthatches.

The materials you need are a 6″×¾″ unplaned board approximately 4′ 9″ long, two dozen 1½″ nails, a few tacks and a 6″×2″ strip of rubber or waterproof canvas. The tools you need are: a saw, a hammer and something to make the hole.

Cut the board in lengths as shown. The slopes of the two Sides are formed by the one diagonal cut. The width of the Base is 4½″ for exactly ¾″ thick wood (i.e. 6″ minus two thicknesses of wood). The hole should be 1⅛″ in diameter, and can be made by drawing a circle around a 10 pence piece. There are several ways of making the hole: using a drill and large bit, cutting out with a coping saw, or making a small hole and enlarging with a file.

To assemble your box, nail together in this order: one Side to the Back, then Base, the other Side, Front. Before nailing the Front, lay the Roof in position to make sure that the Front does not project too high.

For a hinge use the strip of thick rubber or canvas, nailed (preferably with copper tacks) to the Back and Roof. It is advisable to fix little hooks or clips at both sides of the Roof to hold it down (brass "sidehooks" are best); put the eyes so that the Roof is pulled tight against the Back.

Erect on a tree or post in early spring.

6"
BACK
2"
6"
ROOF
8½"
6"
18"
10"
8"
SIDE
8"
FRONT
SIDE
6"
BASE
6"
4½"

A hide

bird-watching

One great advantage of bird-watching over other pursuits is that so little equipment is required. However, a few items are necessary.

The first is binoculars. Although you can do some bird-watching, particularly in your garden, without binoculars, sooner or later you will need them. The chief function of binoculars is to magnify objects so that they can be seen in greater detail. However, do not suppose that very high magnification is good; generally speaking, the higher the magnification, the heavier and bulkier the binoculars, the more difficult to hold still, and the smaller "the field of view" (the area covered). For young beginners, I recommend 8 × 30. If you can hold larger ones really still and if your bird-watching is mainly on coasts and estuaries, you might find the more powerful 10 × 50 better. Choose binoculars with "central focusing" and "coated lenses". Although makes such as Zeiss and Barr and Stroud are undoubtedly best, they are expensive; I would recommend a good Japanese pair costing £ 8 to £ 15; in particular, the 8 × 30 "Nipole" Japanese binoculars sold by Charles Frank Ltd. (145 Queen Street, Glasgow, C.1.) are excellent value, and the firm will send them on approval and give a seven years' guarantee.

Another essential is a good identification book. The best are *The Hamlyn Guide to Birds of Britain and Europe* and *A Field Guide to the Birds of Britain and Europe*. However, both of them are very comprehensive, and young beginners might start with *The Observers Book of Birds* or even the little *I-Spy Birds*.

You should have a field notebook and pencil to record all your observations as soon as possible after you have made them; this is especially important for the descriptions of any birds you cannot identify.

Wear strong footwear, an anorak and plenty of warm clothing underneath. A map (1 inch Ordnance Survey) and compass are useful and, in mountainous country, essential. As your bird-watching progresses, you may want to add a camera with a telephoto lens, a hide and a portable tape recorder.

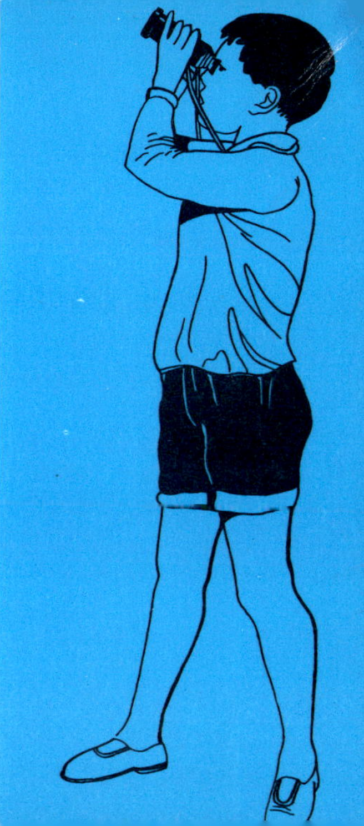

Societies concerned with birds

At national level:

The Nature Conservancy, 19 Belgrave Square, London, S.W.1.

The Royal Society for the Protection of Birds, The Lodge, Sandy, Bedfordshire.

The British Trust for Ornithology, Beech Grove, Tring, Hertfordshire.

The Wildfowl Trust, Slimbridge, Gloucestershire.

The Young Ornithologists' Club, The Lodge, Sandy, Bedfordshire.

At local and regional level:

County Naturalists' Trusts, The Society for the Promotion of Nature Reserves, The Manor House, Alford, Lincolnshire.

Natural History Societies, Bird Clubs, etc. These exist in many towns and districts, and the names and addresses can usually be obtained from your local public library.